Remember the Birds

Remember the Birds
LOUISE C. CALLAGHAN

salmonpoetry

Published in 2005 by
Salmon Publishing,
Cliffs of Moher, County Clare, Ireland
Website: www.salmonpoetry.com
email: info@salmonpoetry.com

Copyright © Louise C. Callaghan, 2005

ISBN 1 903392 51 9

All rights reserved. No part of this publication may be reproduced or transmitted in any form or by any means, electronic or mechanical, including photography, recording, or any information storage or retrieval system, without permission in writing from the publisher. The book is sold subject to the condition that it shall not, by way of trade or otherwise, be lent, resold or otherwise circulated without the publisher's prior consent in any form of binding or cover other than that in which it is published and without a similar condition, including this condition, being imposed on the subsequent purchaser.

Cover artwork: 'Sea Light X' by Bridget Flannery, 2004
Cover Design & Typesetting: Siobhán Hutson

To the memory of my father

Acknowledgments

Acknowledgements are due to the editors of the following publications in which some of these poems first appeared:

Poetry Ireland Review, Issues 70, 74 & 82; *The Stinging Fly*, 2003; *The Irish Times*; *Out to Lunch* Anthology (2002); *Jumping the Bus Queue* Anthology (2000); *World Literature Written in English* (2003); *Forgotten Light: Memory Poems* (2003); *Something Beginning With P: New Poems from Irish Poets* (2004).

The author wishes particularly to acknowledge & thank fellow poets of Thornfield Writing Group.

And I blessed them unaware.
　　S. T. COLERIDGE

Contents

Early Waking	15
Secret	16
'Remember the Birds'	17
The little tray	17
Watersnake	18
Goodbye	19
The Swing	20
Umbelliferae	21
Brothers	22
Inis Meáin	23
Cill Ceannannach	24
Fandango	25
For Holly & Jessica	26
Child Prodigy	27
History Book	28
schoolgirl	28
monk	28
blackbird	29
Ballade	30
The Town Square	31
There Was a Soldier	32
Called to See the Newborn	33
Wish	34
Mortuary	35
Hummingbird in Berkeley	36
Scarlet Macaw	37

Kahlo in Hospital	38
Ways of Mourning	39
Poems	39
Her Life	40
The Wake	41
Mount Venus	42
Epitaph	43
Mistletoe Kiss	44
New Year's Eve	45
Honours	46
Still-Life	47
Pietas	48
Ten Years Ago	50
Happy on the 51 Bus	52
Haunted Places	53
Do you dream of me	54
Lent	55
School Yearbook	56
Skellig Michael	57
In the Boat	57
Bird Sanctuary	58
Pilgrims	59
Monastic Settlement	60
Matins	61
Homage to Anne Le Marquand Hartigan	62

Foal	63
Love Triangle	64
Robin	64
Blackbirds	65
One Magpie	66
The Happiest Moments	67
Burnt Images	68
Soulcase	69
Evening	70

Early Waking

The garden is quiet for July, silent
but for a sole hooded-crow that taps
along the roof-gutters, in search
of worms or ivory-coloured grubs.
And again the muffled cry of a magpie.

Behind glass, early sun shone hot,
the girl curled in her nightclothes,
in the window-seat, reading a book,
withdrawn from the world by curtains.

She must judge each of the stories,
if the macabre twist is true or false.

Secret

I no longer want to
live with my doubts,

always holding back.
It is poetry,

the urge to understand,
be personal too,

tell you something
you might never

otherwise hear,
hold you

with my deepest secrets,
a few words

spark, flare
in the dark

and the whole truth
come out.

'Remember the Birds'

The little tray

In my hall, the walnut console
holds Father's wood-crafted tray,
the flute-lip tidy for assorted keys, letters,
household bills, a bottle of *Rescue*.

That he made it himself never
struck me so much as the motto,
the words he'd chosen to groove
into the surface: *Remember the Birds*

as if there were nothing more
meaningful he could think of;
his dead-pan sense of the absurd.
Remember the Birds: no

philosophy, no moral. I let
my lofty expectations go,
I'll use the little tray for crumbs,
to carry and to scatter them.

Watersnake

    At four, before reason
or measure could rescue me,
I gave up talking to him, at six,
I ran away from home for good
on my sister's two-wheeler.

He taught me to swim
frog-shapes, then butterfly.

He never intervened when Mother
packed me off to boarding school,
(their after-thought was due).
I couldn't read, but worse
I still wet the bed.

My passion for cars and car engines
I learnt from him. Twisted my tongue
around *Traders Magneto Dynamo
Limited*, the Company name —
His sly delight in poetry:

*the bee, the bat, the butterfly.
The corncrake, the watersnake
and the swallow.*

Goodbye

It is thirteen years since I visited
the clairvoyant in her garden flat.
Straight away, the good seer
announced your presence —
standing by my left shoulder.

Could it be...is he your father?
We were not close and I denied
you meant anything to me now.
I had not come for this comfort.
He wants you to know he is sorry...

It is years since you died —
how slowly I defrost.
Sometimes that lily-scent
of your hair-oil perfumes the air.
I see the gesture, your last goodbye.

The Swing
for Jordi

Lasso, then loop
the obliging branch,
weeping willow,
swing for a day.

No burn of rope
on your rump,
a stolen
cushion can't soften.

Legs like oars,
slowly start
to paddle
the foot worn ground...

then higher
and higher
in wide arcs,
treading paths of air

fly, fly
with the wind
as though never
coming home

urge yourself through
bare branches
capture
half the sky.

Umbelliferae

Tall in the ditch
spokes of an umbrella plant,
the florets of *cowparsley*,

ragged outfit they call
Queen Anne's lace
in the States.

Midsummer in the rain
the rank weeds
are sheltering memory —

along mud-paths,
air sharp
with its manly smell.

In a further season
seeds that will dull
our senses.

Brothers

My brother: I'll never say those words,
our mother had no sons. Words on someone else's tongue,
coupled with *older, younger, brave* or *bullying.*
Our mother's favourite. Our father's.

Was it he who taught us to kneel by our beds
and into the dark, call to God?
God bless Mammy; God bless Daddy...
My father fathered five of us, all girls,
never cast a glance back to our non-existent brother.

Heads bowed, faces in our hands,
from the edge of memory — a shadow:
three boys, *his* soldier-brothers:
Joseph, Eugene, Stanie.

Inis Meáin

A single haystack
in a closed field

burnet-rose
that blooms for a day

Meadow-pipit
cuckoo   corncrake

in the dune   tern
nested in nothing

Blackhag cormorant
hanging over the ocean

like a *pucán*
the currach

up-ended
in a sheltering ditch

Glacial erratics
like odd shoes

beached above
harrowing waves

down in the *grike*
caress of maiden-hair

Held water
talking

to rainwater
in endless confession

Miles upon miles
of stone walls.

Cill Ceannannach

The small stone church,
a roofless ruin

its lintel facing west:
an entrance so low,

so narrow,
I'm unwilling to go in.

I circle old ground
avoiding nettles, potholes,

fallen headstones.
The local names

burned by wind
and rain —

a child's too early
death date.

Beneath my feet
a gaping underworld.

Fandango

*In the absence of trees the island birds
nest in walls of limestone rock.*

I ramble the lane
between dry-stone walls,
tune in to a high-pitch squeak,

prepare to see something
tiny, needy
in the grassy ditch:

four open mouths,
diamond-shape,
edged with yellow.

Along the top of the wall,
a wren dances
to distract me,

decoy of hop and song.
Wing-tail cocked
like a closed fan

a warning.

For Holly & Jessica

A wooded area
in ground edged by August
fields after harvesting

two little girls
in shallow graves,
under cover of leaves.

Through hourly news-reports
I follow a towpath
along wet Fenland meadows,

remembered its silences,
those wide horizons
far from the sea.

Child Prodigy
for Susan Connolly

It is seven years since Breifne flew
out through the tall floor-to-ceiling window
of your eighteenth-century house.
He was in practising the piano, his own
composition, or maybe that *rum-ti-tum-*
tum of Samba music he'd improvised
on a biscuit tin all that Summer.
A toy lying on the floor tripped him,
he ended this head-over-heels career
through unresisting air out on Fair Street,
between parapet and spiked iron railings,
in the basement-well of Number 22.
You flew to him, Xena-like, in three and
four stair-leaps, a puff of stars at your heel.
He revived effortlessly, like a cat,
as its ninth life begins. Cased in plaster
to the hip he went hopping everywhere.

History Book

schoolgirl

In my school-book
before I could read

I gaze at one woodcut,
its blacks and grays —

all I want is
to fill that page with colour.

monk

At my work
copying

gospel Latin,
quill tipped in ink,

a poem chased
across the page

headlong
to the margin.

blackbird

At daybreak —
the intensity of song,

a blackbird
in the whitethorn:

the title-page
of dawn.

Ballade

Slow, hesitant, the notes
searched for on the keys
remind me of my sister. Long ago,
how she practised at the piano.
For hours, her back to the world,
head forward, hands reaching
for grace in each note.
A lonely, striving sound.
My sister's face at birth,
blemished by a mole
it was removed, and later
when she'd finished growing,
the puckered scar.
As fingers find their way,
the music starts to flow.

The Town Square

Poppies blood the fields,
droop-head
for the imperturbable dead.

In the distance, *Albert*,
a toppled spire, once suspended there
not by any miracle, a thread

of twisted cable
held the Mother & Child
from falling into the Square.

Boy-soldiers everywhere,
on both sides of the great River
record a statue dancing on limned air.

There Was A Soldier

for my sisters A.H.; G.P.; M.B. and J.R.

The village was nothing
more than the *Mairie*,
a couple of red-roof barns
and a street of facing houses.

But the air was marvellous,
the roads unchoked
by marching men
or machinery.

I walked on out
towards *Bouzincourt*,
to the British Cemetery.
A cloudless sky

stretched over fields,
the curves and capes
of no-man's-land.
Silver-grey arrows

going south to the coast,
dissipated vapour-trails
unfolding like bales
of barbed-wire fence.

Among the tended graves
I found his number:
Royal Munster Fusilier,
wings of eagle crest.

When death came piping
over Picardy
he was never to be
a father, nor an uncle.

Called to See the Newborn

Her dark head is crowned
in a tangle of wires   tabs

clipped to her forehead   and there
at her un-breasted nipple

Ribs of her heaving chest
where there is never

enough air   Skin   livid
puffed-up   with fever

but you notice her feet
and hands are perfect,

their tiny half-moons like lotus,
like floating petals.

Wish

Like the first page
of a storybook
torn clean
of its life

like the last dream
to burst colourfully
then slip away
as you wake

and this wish
for the L
of her name
to be mine.

Pietas

My father has gone
but a ghost lives on

in the white-washed house.
Pulled from the shadow,

in their bedroom,
at the bureau mirror

dressing for work.
Silver-back brushes

cleave and gleam
silver-black hair

in fierce unison.
From her side of the bed

mother observes.
He will kneel,

drop a sleeked head
in the hammock of her lap

for his morning prayers.
Eyes housed

in homeless dark
there is no telling then

where he is.

Hummingbird in Berkeley

In the tree-top
plush greenery

the tiniest bird
hovering

a viridian-blue
haiku

its mute notes
for all I know

in too high
a frequency

the imperceptible
whirr of its wings

a sideways pass
to exit backwards

shy little
Madame Butterfly.

Scarlet Macaw

I woke to the faintest tints of dawn
lightening valley dark and there again
in among bird-song I heard it, my macaw,
the unmusical two-note call.
A bird escaped from its caged life
lives in the valley.

Up and down the steep gorge of the *Tramuntana*,
over almond and jacaranda, silver-flowering oleander,
the swaying reeds and towering evergreens;
palms and blossom-scented lemons like a phantom.
Does it yearn for company, or only search
for a way back to an open cage?

The sound will follow me up the narrow
path later, haunting me for a reply.
When I hasten back in the rustling dark
under a vast night sky I must depend on my own
desperate whistle for company.
I imagine it sees the rat in this half-light entering

the chicken hutch, wakening guinea-fowl
from their perched slumber, scuffling
the husk in its search for seed.
And the chestnut mare over on the other side,
in the last untilled terrace of grass — graceful
even as it stumbles up from sleep.

You can never tell where its caw
will come from next. You may never see it.
Leaning from my open window, inhaling
petal-scented air, a shadow of cape-wings
lurches from branch to branch. In the valley
an echo of its half-melodious song.

Kahlo in Hospital

Lying down
with thorns

the twisted vine
for companion

white sheets
her only vista.

The shroudless
skinless

skeleton on top
of the canopy

is Death
her private-eye.

Ways of Mourning
Lily Páircéir, 1 September — 11 October, 2002

Poems

Six weeks
she lived
cupped in our gaze

then grew old
in a night,
aged in pain.

Kiss her
goodbye,
bury her tomorrow.

    ★

We kiss her forehead
over and over
with unspoken words,

on a half-ready hillside
leave her
to bell-heather,

birdsong, aerial
views of the city
where we are gone.

    ★

Heads bowed,
as one
we came down:

the small boy howling,
her brother,
gave a voice to our sorrow.

Her Life

In a glass incubator
Instead of in a cradle

In our gaze twice daily

In the hospital   its
Intense lighting and unnatural air

Intrusive procedures   handled
        with deft care

        She is often
In pain   Her mother in despair

    Resuscitated one more time

In the night   her parents   holding her

In their arms
        the first hour after midnight
            when she died

In the ante-room   see her   wrapped
In Ruth's pink shawl

In her own home
        Candle-lights flicker

In turns   watched   Waked

In the white coffin now
In their car
        Carried on her father's knee

In the open grave

In these palaces of the mind   She is
Indelible

The Wake

Can't someone bring her back
you want to know, and cast
a boy's age-of-reason eyes
from one to another of us.
At her side you start a sketch:
her face-bones, the bare
dainty stillness of winter birch,
crease of pencil-marks perfectly
resembling folds of soft skin,
sunken at each temple where
bruise-coloured, blood has risen,
an eye-lid half open.
Life haunts the likeness.
This is how we'll remember her.

Mount Venus

Silence is no stranger up here
above *Bohernabreena*.
Each return is to be alone,
not really thinking of anything:

to see the flight pattern
birds make, a *V*
and every few minutes
a jet-trail milking the sky.

The absence of trees
is planned, the havoc of roots,
not to disturb our dead.
I like thinking of you

on your own up here with
and without your daughter.
Then dark, the gusting air,
another shooting star's departure.

Epitaph

It is six months to the day.
Dark clods of earth, clay
soft with rain

await a headstone.
Her name, the dates,
all that will be known of her.

I will mourn her,
little granddaughter
with wisps of air.

Mistletoe Kiss

A tangled branch hooked
down from some tall tree
this edge of winter,

whose root
clung to an unknown host
bared of all leaves,

pearl-drop berries,
seeds buried in a haze
of see-through liquid,

curls of greenest leaf.
Below this sprig
hung from the crossbeam,

fir-scent of woodland,
someone kissed me —
lips unseen by anyone.

After months of silence
a song sent to me
from the forest.

New Year's Eve

These last scant hours,
mortality's time when souls
overflow, want to be heard:

the moon in a clearing
recalls for you too, I'm sure of it,
dear nights of bliss. And beyond

the dark of dark's enclosure.
The new year, hidden from view,
we cannot call home.

Alone or not alone,
we walk into the shadow
of what is to come.

Honours

i.m. Margaret Lefranc, 1907-1998

At birth
we receive our breath's
full regalia,

heart drumming
the anthem it has already
come to love —

now as then
our lives governed
by the same air.

But when night winds fail,
shadows lengthen
on the wall,

someone will watch
a flame
cease to flicker.

Still-Life

i.m. Dorothy Molloy

In a small room,
life is crowding in on them.

That afternoon
at the Exhibition to view

columns and gyres, vertebrae
swaddled in ticking, or tapestry:

for richer, for poorer.
And the human form

with stitches rising each seam.
Where there is no title

we rely on the date.
I want only the hour,

the minute of extinction,
when the one now desolate

doubled over her, in tenebrae,
the awful leave-taking.

The fruit fruitful, the flower…

January 4th, 2004

Mortuary

i.

In her eighty-seventh year
the *king of her heart* gave out,
small organ, in China
called the mightiest.
No bigger than your own fist,
see it, pen-clenched like this.

ii.

White-haired my father-in-law
in the hospital stiff chair;
chapel light and scentless air.
Where we are afraid to look
yet we still want to look
at her laid out in the coffin.

iii.

Across from me   the man
at his father's shoulder stands guard

guarding whatever it is he guards
Husband   estranged

as long as we once were married
face I no longer read

We speak but our eyes
seldom meet

I feel a separateness
a rush of tears

as if seized by first grief
In the exact light

in the silent waiting-room
not death I see

nor side-face   his bowed father
but us as we might have been.

Ten Years Ago

i

I am told daideo
you are eighty-four today.
I remember when you asked me
if we'd have a roll in the hay.
A separated woman would be lonesome.

It was a different story that Sunday.
I saw you behind my pew
down on one knee, head bowed,
your bare crown, a penitent.
Wasn't it well I said no.

ii

His beauty astonished me that day
raking hay,

turning the second cut,
dismantled worlds between us —

the way he set aside stones
from the wall

to enter and to leave the small
arena of his closed field,

or like a seagull that lifts
suddenly to wheel

further west
out over the Sound.

iii

I sometimes wondered
where we'd go
for our love act

hardly on top
of the one haycock
in the middle of his tiny field.

I imagine waiting for him
under a hedge, fuchsia's
scarlet-skirted bells,

and going with him around
the back of the island
where there'd be no-one,

nothing only stones, boulders.
And as darkness fell
the unlikely unbuttoning.

iv

First I noticed the new bike
resting in the ditch,
a gift from his family in England

and not far from it,
rambling across fissured table-rock,
him with his sheepdog.

Winter-coated, small against the sky,
driftwood bundled under his arm,
he raised his cap with his free hand.

Happy on the 51 Bus

Fairylights trail the hungry trees
long after maple leaves
decompose in the gutter. Blooms
of magnolia like the big-figure

black women who crowd this bus.
And our driver who drums the blues,
improvising on the steering-wheel:
A'm the best driver they got!

Oakland folk all talk to one another.
The homeless mutter — hurl
vacant or raging eyes. Opposite,
short lyrics up among the ads.

Haunted Places

In a culvert they tracked
the bundled clothes: a muddied blouse,
stockings rent at the crotch,
one black shoe, its heel collapsed.

Elsewhere, somewhere are packed
the naked body parts that fit her
description — Pale, pale skin
underneath smothering clay.

The silence at home is
what her parents notice and say
to a news reporter when asked.
Her smile vanished months ago

flung into eternity.
Still I yearn for some further
desecrated detail, unable to stop
myself, unable to let her go.

Do you dream of me

Not in the realm we generally meet
of telephone calls, small talk,
or a brief salute on a crowded street,
you with your wife, your daughter.

We spend time together in my dreams.
After all these years you, unappeased
or so you seem. Sometimes
I wonder if you dream of me.

Waking to dark skeletal trees,
I grasp at last night's dream: by the sea,
among marram-grasses we sit at ease
in swathes of summer light.

Lent
for Julie

It wasn't proper to drink milk
on Good Friday. Food
wasn't meant for pleasure.
Herring, its fine little hair-like
bones stuck in your throat,
for a child quite frightening.
Down steps to the pantry
for eggs, softened shells afloat,
preserved all through Winter
for the hot-cross buns.

School Yearbook

I keep turning to his photo, the posed
face of my sister. A boy-soldier
home on leave. His last look.
The story goes of him arrested,
held over Easter in the Four Courts.
Ice winds ploughing up the Liffey.
Insurgents as young as himself,
among ruins, crouched in a door.
Any one of them could be
from his class in school.
The contradictory clatter of war
sounding off the cobbled quays.

Skellig Michael

He who knows how cruel is sorrow for a companion
understands: the paths of exile claim him.*
The Wanderer

In the Boat

Rock companion for Little Skellig, three-
quarters of an hour out from Portmagee.

Our boat like a shell on the sea,
motor-propelled it rose and fell.

Boatman and me. The petticoat-swell
of a million sun-tipped waves.

Bird Sanctuary

        To
      our left
    like a ship,
  deck upon deck
  of shining, dark rock.
Hanging mid-air like piano notes:
 gannet, storm-petrel, guillemot.
Cliff-face graffiti. Ancient city of birds

Pilgrims

I start the climb,
an ascent the boatman said
of six hundred steps.
Think heavenwards.

Seabirds in pairs
everywhere,
the only flower
a white-petal pannier.

Back and forth
the rock-laid path;
a stop for breath.
The sea below, slow

waves tipped in sunshine.
Climb and listen,
test the air.
Halfway there, footsteps,

names drop down to me:
Aristotle, Socrates, first causes,
like bell-notes.
We nod on passing.

Monastic Settlement

The Seafarer, The Wanderer, epithets
for solitude. I stair my way up
under a *lux aeterna* sky, stoop to enter:

Six cell houses — each one room for one,
a roofless chapel, and almost human, a standing stone.
As far West as one can go. Notched on the edge of dawn.

* From the early or Old English poem; author unknown. "Wat se pe cunnad/ hu slipen bid sorg to geferan/ pam pe him lyt hafad leofra geholena: / warad hine wraeclast." (trans. L.C.C.)

NOTE: Skellig meaning pinnacle and 'splinter'. And, according to *Dineen's Dictionary*, Michael is patron saint of high places. This rocky Crag, he says, was the Christian scene of pilgrimage and wife selection customs etc.

Matins

Eye-coloured blue
flower

whose name
escapes me:

In a gale
at daybreak, frail

grass-like stem,
bell like the bell

which summoned monks
to first prayer.

And then I remember.

Homage to Anne Le Marquand Hartigan
on her birthday

How I admire people like you
who do all the things you want to do.
Mistress of countless arts!

I saw you last on the steps
of the National Library overlooking the Dáil,
under the full brim of a summer

straw-hat (laced by yourself with tulle)
among porticoes and plump pillars
on Bloomsday — We are invited each year.

You recited in verse for us,
announced your cure for insomnia.
To *Barnacles & Book-keepers*, to readers,

literati of all kinds, to the Nation:
It is poetry and masturbation. Generous
author of poems and paintings and plays,

composer of friendships, of children, and
of children's children to the third generation...
You were never afraid to warm a bed with your poem

equally, not afraid to dart the venom
of your *long tongue*, naming the Furies
when others wished to silence us. Us women.

Creative laureate, voluptuary, teach me
not to lie down.

Foal

A memory   singular
star-like burns

from afar
it falls towards you

a forgotten light
A chestnut mare

alone in the meadow
when you turned once more

no time   no hour

the foal unfolding
from long-ago grass.

Love Triangle

Robin

When cock-robin calls
she comes to him.
Lately there's been no sign

of her. She used to hop
in and out, eat from
my palm. Her trifid feet

like the wild violets
threaded under the trees.
A sweet-toned treble.

Blackbirds

The perplexities of sex are revealed
outside my bedroom window. The blackbirds,
three in all, spring in short steps, in flurries
swoop from ivied wall to the apple-tree;
among failing sprays of my forsythia —
to the propped-up lilac, over, over and back;
the ritual more an obsession.
Spring wearying now, there are just the two.
The jet-eyed one, handsome as a film star
ruffles up a size. While slighter
and more brunette than black the other
verges on hysteria. All you hear
are tenored trills, in turn fluttered shrieks.
Spring holds them tangled in the ancient tree,
victim to its tricks. Nor have I seen
the vanquished one in over three weeks.

One Magpie

A single magpie balances on my side
of the garden wall. Piebald,

swaggering. Hardly a good sign:

a magpie busy thieving sticks,
can it foretell, will she be back?

The Happiest Moments

Over the granite wall seemed like mounting the rump of
 a friendly pony. Big
drop the other side. We jump onto compacted mud
 in among ditch weeds
whose overpowering stink reminds me of the scent of
 our parents' unmade bed

and thrust them aside to find the snake-path running
 deep between
cowparsley's nodding heads; wood-anemone too shy
 for light.
Along the embankment, impressive, still, the rising
 tree-trunks...

We kneel to remove our shoes and school-socks,
 remove winter
garments of stuffy rooms and influenza. The feel of
 bare feet,
the air reanimate pale legs under the material of our
 plaid skirts.

Cuckoo-calls, further and further apart, now stop.
 The Chestnut
holds out its branch-arm to us, a sticky bud. Trees
 determine everything:
who can step, who can sing, who can enhance the wind.

Burnt Images

His figure, but especially his face
etched in a few lines
on a remembered landscape —
collecting strap-wrack, sea-rod.

Wind-blown seagulls, his black dog,
the minutiae scratched and scraped
onto limestone table-rock,
as if bitten into sheet metal.

At low-tide down by the shore,
against ocean light,
a harvest of rods bundled up for kelp.
Salt corrosive in his palm.

Indoors he is no more
than a sedentary person,
he loses the small grandeur fields
and stonewalls impart.

In the church each Sunday,
at the back, crouched
on one knee, he is
mocked for a sinner —

like one of the pilgrims
out of Goya's black painting.

Soulcase

for Lara

In the framer's workshop, the basement,
we stood among frames stacked against every wall,
paintings on canvas, on board behind glass.
I talked out my latest business,
while you two waited all eyes.

After the crazy street, the air, cool as a morgue.
You pulled your little brother in to see —
tucked behind layers three deep,
a small box-frame picture
containing a baby's woollen cardigan.

Pinned like a butterfly.
Too small for a new-born,
not worn more than once or twice,
then washed too hot. It was perfect,
a tiny rosebud motif near each shoulder seam

knotted in a green leaf. Purl/plain, purl/plain:
the ripple of wool through learning hands.
Neither of you spoke a word
as if remembering your infant sister.
Her airless coffin settled on the mountain-side.

Evening

Robins swoop
over dry-stone walls
greet the passersby.

Inadvertent, shy
a tiny wren
will dart for cover.

At twilight, swallows
pilot a curve
like scud-missiles,

sea-gulls,
in from the sea,
rose-coloured with dusk.